FULFILLMENT

A Book of Verse

A Book of Verse
by
Religious of the Cenacle

MCMLVI

J. S. Paluch Co., Inc.
Chicago

Cum permissu superiorum
Nihil Obstat

Reverend Joseph M. Egan, S. J.

Imprimatur

† Samuel Cardinal Stritch
Archbishop of Chicago
Feast of Our Lady of the Cenacle
May 12, 1956

Library of Congress Catalog Card Number: 56 - 11845

To

Our Lady of the Cenacle

Contents

Paschaltide

Archdiocese of Chicago
Chancery Office
719 No. Wabash Ave.
Chicago 11, Illinois

June 15, 1956

My dear Sisters,

I thank you very much for sending me your manuscript, FULFILLMENT. These little poems are precious gems and tell in beautiful language the thoughts and sentiments of souls near to God. In returning this manuscript to you I want to express my appreciation of it and express the hope that what the authors long for and pray for may be obtained by all who read this book.

With best wishes,

Sincerely yours in Christ,

+ Vane bam Vhm

Archbishop of Chicago

The Religious of the Cenacle
Convent of Our Lady of the Cenacle
513 Fullerton Parkway
Chicago 14, Illinois

Foreword

Medieval craftsmen did not chisel the perfection of the Madonna until they had mastered design, had learned the intricacies of the acanthus. The dedicated artist does not attempt the idea until he has mastered the form.

It is with joy that one lights upon such dedication, such mastery. The Religious of the Cenacle possess, of course, those divine concepts which they have learned at the altar. But they have been unsatisfied with the bare poetic idea. They have had an appreciation that a poem is *a thing made,* a perfect thing, and that the chiseling, the modeling, the apprenticeship to techniques, is a part also of their tribute to God and our Lady.

It is not infrequently that one finds a great artist in the convent. Many have been such. But it is rare indeed, when so many, in a single Congregation, coming from so many different places and local cultures, can show that consistency of high achievement which is discoverable in this volume.

I praise this book for all its values. Above all, I praise it as a proof of that principle of the Cenacle Religious, that what one does for God, one does excellently. Like all their work, like all art, this is indeed the well-doing of that which is to be done.

John L. Bonn, S. J.

Season of Advent

"The Lord is now nigh,
Come, let us adore Him."

Matins: Invitatory

"Exspectans, exspectavi Dominum..."

PSALM XXXIX

David, you are a man of song. Your soul
Is vibrant with the majesty you sing.
Isaias, you have the lips God cleansed with coal,
Fire-tipped and pure the promises they bring.

Precursor John, you are the voice that dies
Sounding the advent of the Living Word
Across the wilderness with mighty cries.
No greater prophet ever will be heard.

But, Mary, I shall wait for Christ with you,
Whose *fiat* seals the covenant of peace.
You are the rainbow and the freshening dew
That wakens man to sureness and release.

O hope, heaped high as waters in the sea,
Break, break upon my heart's expectancy.

Catherine Carney, r.c.

Alma Redemptoris Mater

Was it Mary's stainless soul
That brought God from above,
Was it all the years of longing,
Or was it simply Love?
O Tabernacle pure
Of the justice-mercy kiss,
Enfold us all within
Thy womb of darkest bliss.
Ah! There we'll learn our loving
With Incarnate Love unknown.
Oh! Mother, bring us forth
To live . . . by Him alone.

Gretchen Funck, r.c.

Longing

The Virgin longed to see the face
Of Him she bore. She, full of grace,
Must wait nine months to gaze upon
Her God, her Christ, her Son.
At last, O ever-mounting joy,
He's born — her Boy!
And lo, His sacred baby features
Are like one other creature's;
His lips, His eyes, His brow,
Formed in her till now,
Are but her own,
Hers, hers alone.
The longing, is it stilled?
Ah no, for God hath willed
Unto eternity
Her task should be
To mold His features once again,
This time within all men.

Agnes Vollmann, r.c.

Lone Way to Jericho

In wordlessness the Word of God is seen,
Against the foliage of void He flowers.
The way that leads to Him is hid in green,
Green having-nothing that avers Him ours.
Adventurous, with Eden's bridges down,
Burnt down by swirling seraph, we must turn,
Each Adam, Eve, each Lot of some small town,
Some house which, Mary-mantled, did not burn:
Bend down and find adventure in this room,
Within this moment shelled, unseal from time
A pearl, a song, a sixpence, a perfume,
From voicelessness a vision frail, sublime:
To dearth, to bareness bend, as God has bent,
Create, discover, lavish on the dull
Whose jewel, fragrance, hope's last song, last cent
Was robbed, two alms, the good, the beautiful.
Forever Love leaps down to littleness
That dared (and fell) the lone way walled in green.
All golden orchards wave in His caress.
In wordlessness the Word of God is seen.

Winifred Corrigan, r.c.

"Veni . . ."

(A Little Way of the Cross)

I. Come, Thou, Word, in silence living,
II. Come, Thou, Fullness, ever giving.
III. Come, Omnipotence, bent low,
IV. Come, O Love, through sorrow flow,
V. Come, O Strength, with weakness laden,
VI. Come, Thou, veiled by Advent's Maiden.
VII. Come, Thou, Dew from heaven, falling,
VIII. Come, O Mercy, heed our calling.
IX. Come, Humility Divine,
X. Come to swaddling bands all mine.
XI. Come, the stable has its cross,
XII. Come, Repairer of man's loss.
XIII. Come, Little One, to Mary's arms,
XIV. Come and quiet Death's alarms.

Clare Gartland, r.c.

The Annunciation

The radiance of the little room grew dim.
The angel's message, now a memory deep,
Too deep for aught save silent pondering love,
Was folded in her valiant heart to keep.

There was a next day — silently she went
Her daily round of tasks as other days.
But ah! How changed for singing in her heart;
The Word was making music down her ways.

Isabelle O'Leary, r.c.

10

Christmastide

"Christ is born unto us;
Come, let us adore."

Matins: Invitatory

Christmas

O luminous hour, when day pierced
night
To find on the altar of Mary's
breast
The Taper of Infinite
Light.

Lucille Lang, r.c.

God's Little Cradled Word

Within His eyes are mirrored
His Mother's eyes and smile,
And all the angels marvel
Above His crib the while.

He is the Lord Eternal,
Though born but yesterday.
He sees those kneeling near Him,
And hears them when they pray.

To some He gives a shining thought
To light the coming year;
To others, cherubs' gladness,
In knowing Heaven's near.

Yet though He lies in silence,
His thundering voice is heard
Throughout creation's vastness —
God's little cradled Word!

Louise Manning, r.c.

The Night

Had the moon been a cradle of light
The night
That Christ was born in Bethlehem,
Would Our Lady have let it hang on high
In the midnight of a winter sky
To lay
The new-born Lamb of God
On hay?
Ah, yes!
Would angels on their star-dust way
Have heard the whispering moonlight say
Its ray
Was beam of welcome
Come from crib of gold
As old
As time?
Ah, no!
Would Mother all holy, or angels all bright
Have heeded the waning boast of night,
When they beheld Eternal Light
In swaddling clothes?

Clare Gartland, r.c.

Song for a Mother

O Patrick's fire
And Roland's horn,
Hush till my babe
Is truly born.

O Abraham, be
Thy feasting screened
Until the child
Is really weaned.

O lamps of Prudence,
Yet be trimmed
Until the blue
Young eyes are dimmed.

And God distends
The womb of earth
And spirit stirs
To nobler birth

And Eve lies still
Past pain and hap
And Abel crows
In Mary's lap

And saints rejoice
And angels laugh:
Then I the christening
Wine may quaff

And Christ shall smile
With me and say:
"A child is born
To Us today".

Winifred Corrigan, r.c.

Jesus' First Step

Come, Love, come now to Mother's arms!
  Put out those little feet!
Thy father watches, Thy Mother's near,
  My Lovelet, come, my Sweet!

A tiny sandal treads the floor,
  A second — then the bliss
Of the all-but-heaven of every babe,
  His Mother's arms and kiss.

Louise Manning, r.c.

The Rubber Cat

I

The April of his child-like eyes
Was troubled with December skies.

He listened while his mother told
Of Christ in a manger, wintry cold.

"O Mother, where was His little bed?
Where the pillow for His head?"

"Unless He cradled on Mary's breast
On the manger's straw would Jesus rest."

"Where was His blanket, soft and fine?
Where were His sheets all white like mine?"

"The white snow blanketed all the earth
And the ox-breath warmed the Savior's birth."

II

A tear stood bright on the baby's cheek;
With tear-choked voice he began to speak,

"If I give Him my bed, will you begin
With Mother Mary to tuck Him in?"

Holding him close, the mother smiled
Tenderly on her little child.

"Too late, too late to give to Him,
Sheltered now by the Seraphim.

But there are many children here,
Dear to Christ, and very dear;

And if your gifts you give to them,
You give to the Babe of Bethlehem."

18

III

A smile came over the little lad's face.
He brought his toys from their heaped-up place,

And drums and soldiers, tops and rings,
He gave to the Child all kinds of things.

And when the shining pile was done,
He had given them all—yes, all save one.

He thought all day, "My toys were new,
But this is bent and broken, too.

It's only a little old rubber cat."
Surely the Lord would leave him that.

Surely the Lord would let him keep
The comfort he clasped each night in sleep.

IV

But then with his treasure close in bed,
He thought of what his mother said.

The Holy Child for love of him
Was alone in a stable in Bethlehem.

The bright tear stopped on his rounded cheek,
To hear what the shining angels speak

To shepherds and kings and little boys,
"Come, bring me your sheep and gold and toys!"

And rising quickly he went to where
His bright toys heaped, and crying there

He threw down his dear and rubber cat,
And said aloud, "Here, Lord, take that!"

Gertrude Morton, r.c.

19

Your Christmas in New Zealand

Though summer blooms break out on all your hills
And radiant skies arch over flowering vine,
Though gulls dip soft and low by summer seas
And grapes are reddening for your Advent wine,
The same small Child Who comes to us in snows
On frosty nights with stars hung clear and high,
Comes down to you as dew upon soft grass,
When summer clouds dream in a summer sky.
His love holds all the seasons in its clasp,
And trace of little feet mark every land.
For you, a bluebell blossoms by His crib,
For us, a snowflake glistens in His hand.

Isabelle O'Leary,r.c.

20

The Beloved Disciple

Come, John, so ends your liebestraum. Arise.
Forsake the golden bough's divinest rest,
Stir like a waking child against His breast,
Behold the sea of sorrows in His eyes.
Have not the years' stern training taught you this:
Not for yourself that flight beyond the sea,
You must return when you have found the tree
As did the chosen dove of Genesis.

You must go solitary and apart,
Forever marked with mysteries of pain,
Bearing the brief commission to remain,
And draw the world to rest upon His Heart,
Until it cries beneath the weight of grace,
"O Christ, O Christ, O Christ, to see Thy face!"

Margaret Byrne, r.c.

My Life with Jesus
(St. Bernard)

All my life is Jesus,
'Tis passed beneath His gaze,
When sleeping, 'tis of Him I dream,
He fills my nights and days.
I study, Jesus teaches.
I write, His hand guides mine.
'Tis Jesus Who writes "Jesus",
His Name, on every line.
When walking, He walks with me,
I sit, He sits close by.
When praying, He prays in me,
'Tis He Who prays, not I.
When tired, Jesus rests me,
And when I feel alone,
He takes my heart and puts it
In a corner of His own.
For me to live is Jesus,
To die is all the same,
The only life I know of
Is found in that sweet Name.

Isabelle O'Leary, r.c.

Epiphany

The star without was great and high,
And outshone every other;
The Star within was infantine,
And cradled in Its Mother.

Lucille Lang, r.c.

The Star Is Still

The star is still, burning with tranquil heat.
Those desert nights we watched its moving fire
Are gone like sand beneath the camels' feet.
We stand upon the threshold of desire.

Where is the king we left our land to find?
The streets of Bethlehem are dark and chill.
We leave the dreaming town a league behind —
Is there a lantern on that distant hill?

The centuries whirl by unheralded.
What hour is this, what world? Oh, time and space
Have opened on a cave God-tenanted.
Eternity lights up a Baby's face!

Heaven comes down to earth, and earth ascends.
Divinity cries out, "You are My friends."

Eileen Surles, r.c.

In Nazareth

My thoughts went down to Nazareth
With lowly duties just like mine.
I knelt before my daily task
With folded hands as at a shrine.

Isabelle O'Leary, r.c.

Prayer in Strife

O Mother, when may we hail thee
As *Our Lady of Release?*
In Cana-wise, come, give us glance
And say, "They have no peace."

Clare Gartland, r.c.

Season of Lent

" Let it not be in vain for you to rise
up early before the light:
For the Lord has promised a crown
to those who watch. "

Matins: Invitatory

O Restless Heart

I loved You always. It was You I sought
Alone at night in a wild untraveled wood,
Driven by needs beyond the leap of thought,
Old to the heart but little understood.

I glimpsed Your lantern once between the trees
And caught its dim reflection in a pool,
But brambles brought me sharply to my knees,
While Pain unwound her darkly-gleaming spool.

I heard Your voice, I heard You speak my name.
Groping my way across uneven ground,
Forcing my passage like a stubborn flame,
I searched for You, but could not trace the sound.

I paused. A branch rustled, a twig broke,
And then I saw You moving through the night
With lifted head and widely-blowing cloak.
You crossed a narrow brook, You raised Your light,

You turned and drove through my heart like a
                    plunging sword
The eyes of God. My Lord, my Lord, my Lord!

Eileen Surles, r.c.

Isaian Moment

*"For a small moment have I forsaken thee: but with
great mercies will I gather thee."*   Isaias LIV

I have a Thabor vision in my heart,
Christ. Send me onward to the cloud-swirled peak.
Frail child am I, yet brave enough to start
Bold climbing toward the Beauty that I seek.

In the Upper Room with Thee I have been fed,
Christ. Lead me now to barren, wasted lands.
Made strong by chaliced Wine and taste of Bread
I can go singing over burning sands.

Such was my prayer before the searching years
Began. Long have I tarried at the mountain's base
All fear. For food and drink I have but tears;
Songless, I am myself the desert place.

Small moment of forsaking this? I wait.
Come, come, Love, gather me with mercies great.

Catherine Carney, r.c.

In Whatsoever Guise

Humiliation is your beggar's hood,
It hides the royal head, yet I can tell
The crown, shining like sunlight in a wood.
I know you in this masking. All is well.

And desolation is a cloak you wear.
The royal garments cast too sure a spell
To be a test of love. And yet I swear
I know you in this garb. Oh, all is well.

Pain is a sword you do not fear to use,
Striking too swift to say if it be Hell
Or Heaven in the thrust. Yet I can choose.
I know whose wrist is agile. All is well.

Come to me, Lord, in whatsoever guise,
I shall be waiting with exultant eyes.

Eileen Surles, r.c.

Temptation Conquered

Christ does not will to make a loaf
  But form a cornerstone;
He wills to feed the multitude,
  Not break His bread alone.

Divinity's unfathomed zeal
  Will be content to wait
For *bread,* not stones, as element
  To transubstantiate.

Lucille Lang, r.c.

Adoration: Mid-Lent

I kneel at adoration: 'tis mid-Lent.
Like sun before March snow, suspended 'tween
The earth and sky, my soul seeks the Unseen,
Chilled and inert, as if its life were spent.
But see, a spectrum galaxy is bent
Adoring: cobalt iris, shaft of green,
A jonquil gold, magenta tulip's sheen,
Spring's galaxy, a gift all heavensent.
"I am the Life . . ." the Unseen now I see.
My soul, no longer earthbound, catches fire
And all myself is lost to all of me,
Filled yet consumed with infinite desire.
Thou art my Life, my Easter Joy, my Spring,
By Thy sweet Force, this seed to fullness bring.

Alice McConville, r.c.

Jacob's Well

Bold with the assurance of a Saint's endorsement,
I place myself in thought by Jacob's Well.
Off to the east in waves of purple mist
The Hills of Galaad roll through stagnant clouds.
Between the hills the Jordan laps along,
A great green serpent coiling on a bed of blooms.
To the north Mount Carmel sweeps a shimmering
     veil
To the flowery plains of Dothain
Whence Ebal's wooded slope rises and falls,
To the vale where Jacob's Well
Gathers the cooling streams
That flow from Carmel's gleaming snows.
To the south Mount Gerizim, castle-crowned,
Ascends in gradual slopes from Sharon's plain of
     roses
And Ephraim's easy climb.
And over all the heat of summer's noon
Hangs like a leaden cope.
Up from the valley
The fragrance of millions of flowers perfumes the
     air,
Narcissus and iris catching the blue of the sea.
Lizards tune up on the warm southern wall of the
     well.
Bees and bright butterflies dart through the air,
And small birds twitter contentedly.
The hush of wonder hangs over it all
And the little hills shout with gladness.
The valleys are covered with corn
And shine in the sun as they sing.
I am alone by the Well.
A Presence draws near,
Sitting by the Well, by me!
The peace that passeth all understanding
Steals over me.

I feel safe, happy, almost laughing!
The shorn lamb is sheltered from the wind,
The chick is under the wings of the hen,
The eaglet is on the eagle's shoulder,
The smoldering flax is blown to a flame,
The lamb is in the Shepherd's arms
By the river of Peace.
I hear the Master speaking with a woman,
"He who drinketh the water that I will give him
Will never thirst.
But the water that I will give him
Shall become in him a fountain of water."
Mount Ebal, Jacob's Well and Gerizim
Fade from my view.
The Presence remains!
The Gift of God!
Not by Jacob's Well, but by a Fount
Whence spring the waters of Eternal Life,
In the shadow of a Host my thirsty soul
Drinks her fill and is set free.
The child is in the Father's arms.

Jesus sat by the Well because
He was weary.
Dear Master, I am sitting here because
I am weary,
Weary seeking for You,
Not on the highways of Samaria
But through the tortuous labyrinthine ways,
Ways choked with thorns and briars
That burrow through the caverns of my soul.
Grant that soon I may find You
In the infinite silence of those unexplored regions
Of beatitude,
Stretching out to limitless horizons
In the depths of my soul.

Isabelle O'Leary, r.c.

In Quiet Silence

Beneath the silver-dipt, enfolding shadows
Of the night,
Christ walks.

When all things rested in a stillness,
And winter night paused midway in its course,
The Eternal Word, sole Image of the Father,
Love-driven, left the courts of Heaven
To give Himself as hostage for mankind.

Each sunlit hour of day would see His labor
For men's souls,
But night, when others turned to healing rest,
Might find Him drawn apart to enter into converse
With His Father.
Unless some need should call—
Be it a human soul in search of peace,
A human body fearing pain—
The cry of anguish was, to Him,
A word of harsh command.

At length His task was done. His longed-for hour
had come.
But in that night, the last before His death,
The Gift of Gifts passed from His heart and hands
To all His own. Beneath the arch of olive trees
He clasped the Will of God.

The sun of midday paled before
The horrors of His death,
And dead men rose in protest.
But there was none to see His triumph. Once more
The shielding wings of night brushed the earth
When from the burial cloths
The Son of God and man stood free.

Though men no more may see Him walk the streets
As in days past,
When work is done and soothing night
Sings to the world its song of blest relief,
To those who watch and love He comes
And speaks,
And touches aching hearts
To bid them rise
In hope and peace to meet another dawn.

Beneath the silver-dipt, deep shadows of the night
Christ walks.

Mary Louise Moore, r.c.

Amor Meus Crucifixus

They crucified my dear Love
    Upon an April day,
And e'er the April sun set,
    They bore His corpse away.

A new tomb in a hillside,
    Where no man yet had lain,
A garden in the springtime,
    Gave shelter to the Slain.

"His sepulchre is glorious,"
    Inspired, the prophet sings.
His death is with the wicked,
    His burial with kings.

His enemies, unwitting,
    A guard of honor set,
They feared His friends would steal Him,
    And spoil their game — and yet,

They brought Him myrrh and aloes,
    In quantities so great,
Not all the Kings of Juda
    Were buried in such state.

They raised the Wail upon Him,
    To Joakim denied,
"Alas! my Lord and Brother!
    Alas! that Thou hast died!"

The mummied lords of Egypt
    Slept on by human art.
He suffered no corruption,
    Not death itself could part

The Manhead from the Godhead.
The High Divinity
Made sacred still the Body
That claimed the bended knee.

He lay, the mightest Conqueror,
Whose banner e'er was furled,
The Founder of an Empire,
Creator of the World.

Was never such a wooing,
Nor bridal morn so fair.
The roses that He gave me,
Had sanguined all His hair.

Was never such a Lover,
Who set at such a price
His spouse, that nought but dying
Could His desire suffice!

Mabel Tottie, r.c.

The Sepulchre of Jesus

The sepulchre of Jesus
Is the quietest place I know,
For there as each day closes,
Unto my Love I go.

I bring Him balm and spices,
And linen white and fair;
I wash the bloodstained Body
And comb the tangled hair.

But on the morrow early,
My Love will give to me
The very selfsame Body
Which hung upon the Tree!

Mabel Tottie, r.c.

Paschaltide

"The Lord is risen indeed, Allehuia."

Matins: Invitatory

Easter Morning

I woke as birds began to sing.
But shame! 'Twas Easter Day!
The heart that should have greeted Him
Was tardier than they!

The gentle ripple of the rain
Was music to my ears,
It fell so soft upon the sward,
As fell the Magdalen's tears.

A pheasant in the covert side
Went chucking to his hen,
For Spring, by God's sweet ordinance,
Continues fair, as when

That radiant Form, among the flowers,
First took His risen way,
And comforted a breaking heart
At dawn on Easter Day!

Mabel Tottie, r.c.

On the Road

The long road stretched ahead
Between two rows of oleanders,
Ribbons of pink across the rolling hills.
The sun, long past its zenith,
Rode on slender bars of golden clouds
Across the western sky.
The long, low hills of the Shephelah
Burned in a violet haze
Like streams of incense smoke
Swung from far-off censers.
Off to the south
The ragged crags and deep ravines of Seir
Reflected the shadows
Within two pilgrim souls,
Whose hearts were like withered husks
After the kernels have been plucked.
All the tender beauty
Of a spring evening on the Judean hills
Spread its feast of loveliness in vain
Before the two disciples;
Their hearts were heavy as they trudged along.
Hopes and dreams lay smoldering
In a thick smoke of fog,
Disillusioned men in a dark world.
In vain they strove to argue themselves
Into possible grounds for hope.
The Light was drawing near but yet
They knew it not.
A Stranger drew up close beside the two,
But though their eyes were held,
A fire burned within their hearts

44

As while they walked
The Stranger pierced the darkness of their minds
With golden shafts of Wisdom from the seers,
From Moses and the Prophets to the One
Begotten in the splendor of the saints
Before the morning star.
Slowly the lights within the village gleamed,
Warning the three of evening's quick approach.
The Stranger looked ahead, to them it seemed
As if to measure distance to be spanned;
But could they let Him go,
This Man Who stirred the first faint spark of hope
Within their hearts?
To let Him go would mean
The setting of the last far star.
"Stay with us for it is growning dark,
The day is now far spent," they urged.
And He went in with them,
The Shepherd with His sheep.
"They knew Him in the breaking of the Bread!"
The flames the Scriptures lighted in their hearts
Fused into the primal Source of White Light
When Jesus took Bread and with His hands
Broke it and fed His lambs.

Dear Lord, the ways are strewn with dead men's
    bones,
Where hearts should be are heavy-weighted stones.
Breathe with Thy Holy Spirit on the dead
And break to the hungry world Thy Living Bread.
The roads that cut across the world today
Are roads to Emmaus — join us on the way!

Isabelle O'Leary, r.c.

The Breakfast

Out on the lakeside in the hush of dawn,
The first hush
Like the caught breath of a child in wonder,
A White Figure is stirring searching the bracken
for thorn.
Dry it must be and scented for fire,
Like incense that rises in vast cathedrals.
The smoke of the fire
Must lift towards the heavens,
Now blushing rose, amber and cobalt.
Down the shore in the chill of the dawning
The bracken is carried, thorn for the burning.
With sensitive hands
That move like the flutter of doves' wings
He places so carefully,
Places so prayerfully
The thorn and the bracken branch.
Each little twig finds its place, finds its meaning,
Harmoniously patterned
Like warp and woof of linen fine-woven.
Fish must be caught in the shoals on the lake shore,
Savory fish for a feast for the children.
Down to the water's edge the White Figure passes,
Down to the waters that leap at His coming.
His hands like two lilies
Rest for a moment
Over the water, then slowly
Into the lake His hands have descended.
Do the fish in the water discern their Creator?
I think like one school they all glide
To the lakeside, eager to be at His bidding
The food for His banquet.

Like a mother at market choosing the best
For the dear children's breakfast,
He picks and He chooses.
Sizzling and crackling they roast on the fire,
Consumed like His heart to be food for His children.
Honey, sun-golden, must flavor the banquet.
Yonder a honeycomb gleams in the bracken,
The bumble bees call to their Maker and know Him.
Dripping sun-golden like sap in red maples,
Honey pours out into hands that are wounded.

Out on the lake the frail barque of Peter
Is tossed on the waves, as she is every moment.
"Lads, cast the net to the right!"
With the order
The sun topped the hillside and poured out its glory.
Gathered-in sunlight gleamed white on the Master.
Music of sound and beauty of vision
Led to John's cry, "'Tis the Lord, 'tis the Master!"
Out of the barque scrambled glad, salty fishermen
On the brink of the shore.
Wonder and awe restrained them a moment,
'Til music is stirring,
"Come laddies, not fearful, come eat of the banquet."

Around the thorn fire like incense ascending,
With salt in the air, crisp dawn in the blending,
Pale gold in the sky, cobalt in the waters,
And dawn winds soft stirring,
Small birds in their coverts:
Such is the setting where children eat salt fish
Served by white hands where a ruby is burning,
Where Peter is questioned and given the mission
To feed little children such banquets unending.

Isabelle O'Leary, r.c.

Mary Magdalen

"In the place where He was crucified there was a garden." ST. JOHN XIX

Dawn winds were stirring in oak and dark olive,
Spears of gold light shattered into
A thousand white stars,
As they broke on gleaming narcissus,
Or burned into blue flame as they tipped
Tall iris.
From stretches of glistening grass
Fragrance of myrrh and aloes,
Swung from small censers,
Perfumed the morning air;
Doves were cooing in ther coverts
And Mary was searching amid all the beauty
For the only Beauty that could ravish
Her heart.
Her eyes were riveted on a tomb
Gleaming under the cypress trees.
Did it remind her of
An alabaster vase
Broken to spill rich nard
On the feet of the Beloved?
Could she break this rock before her
And release the Lily of the Valley
And the Flower of the fields
To fill her life once more with
The fragrance of His Presence?
She would pitch her tent

48

Over against the tomb
And live in memories of the days
When the white Flower of her Love
Gleamed among the shadows of her life
At every turning of her paths.
Such were her thoughts that golden Paschal morning.

Out of the opalescent dawn suffused with rose,
A burst of song
Broke into a thousand melodies
And floated down the vales of time
To die away on infinite horizons
Beyond the everlasting hills.
"Mary."
"Rabboni."
In the hush of the morning air, so calm, so fair, so
    bright,
A thousand years were as one day,
And one day as a thousand years,
Folded within two words.

Isabelle O'Leary, r.c.

"Exsultet Terra"

Laetentur caeli, exsultet terra.
    Exsultet! Joy is in the air!
Terra tremuit et quievit.
    Alleluia is our prayer.

Death and Life have met in conflict,
    Life won out triumphantly;
For Christ is Life and Christ is God —
    To Him belongs the victory.

Exsultet! Let us all rejoice.
    Alleluia let us sing
On this joyous Resurrection
    Of our Savior and our King.

Mary Angela Roduit, r.c.

The Good Shepherd

Little lamb, why did you wander
    Far away from field and fold,
Far away to unknown pastures,
    Where the grass is parched and old;
Where no gleaming lilies blossom
    By pure streams and brooklets clear,
Where no shepherd keeps his vigil,
    When the stealthy wolf is near?

Worn and weary, I have sought you,
    Little lamb, My long-lost love;
Mountain passes have not kept Me,
    Floods below nor storms above.
Through ravines of deepest danger,
    In the scorching midday sun,
Through the blackest shades of midnight,
    I have sought you, little one.

Isabelle O'Leary, r.c.

The Little Shepherd

(For a little boy)

O little Boy Jesus,
  Come blow Your horn,
Your sheep are so scattered,
  So tired, so torn.

They need their Good Shepherd.
  If only they'd hear
The sound of Your voice,
  It's really so clear!

Please help us, Boy Jesus,
  Your love to impart,
That Your sheep may be led
  To the Fold of Your Heart.

Janet Coffey, r.c.

The Sacristan

I am a shepherd,
Not of lambs that frisk on grass,
Not of sheep that slowly pass
Through wicket gates at eve.
I am a shepherd,
Not of the kind whose cares can cease
When the flocks are herded in folds at peace
As night's dark shadows weave.

I am a shepherd whose cares are vast,
Whose vigilance watches when night has passed,
Whose tireless feet climb the hills unshod,
I shepherd the Lamb of God.

Isabelle O'Leary, r.c.

You Are My Shepherd

I am not troubled, if I follow You.
I am serene and still. You are the Way.
There is no night I can not travel through,
Knowing Your lantern burns till break of day.

What shall I suffer from briar and tangled thorn?
Only a stinging pain that will not last.
Your fingers bind the flesh so briefly torn,
Beneath their healing touch, the pain goes past.

Shall I fear the sudden abyss before my feet?
Where ground was firm, there is no ground at all.
But You are beside me swiftly, strong and sweet,
To halt, to hold. You will not let me fall.

You are my Shepherd until time shall cease.
Following You, my Lord, I walk in peace.

Eileen Surles, r.c.

"Ascendit Deus . . ."

Out on the hills a thousand blossoms shake
Their censers, spilling fragrance on the air.
High in their stalls amid the dripping leaves
The songbirds sit to chant their vesper prayer.

The surpliced trees like acolytes stand round,
And lift their snowy tapers to the skies,
As wistful hearted Spring with fingers cool
Prepares earth's altar for the sacrifice.

High o'er the hills in splendor ultimate,
The heavens await their Lord with chants of praise,
Earth gazes up with not too tearful eyes,
Remembering, "I am with you all your days."

Isabelle O'Leary, r.c.

The Ring Song

(Melody: Jesus, the Very Thought of Thee)

Out in the world long years ago
Our Lord said, "Follow Me,"
And when I faltered, " 'Tis too hard,"
He whispered, "Come and see.
Come, leave the passing things of earth,
And in My house abide,
And I will wed thee with My ring
And make of thee My bride."

And so I made His house my home,
His will my love and life,
His bleeding Heart my strengthening balm
In every ache and strife;
And so I came to dwell within
The palace of the King—
His little handmaid learning how
To wear her Master's ring.

Up shining steps He beckoned me,
The stairway of the throne.
He bade me mount them one by one
And so be more His own;
And at each step new pledge He gave
Of this, "the better part",
His Mother's beads along my side,
His Cross upon my heart.

But now today the time is past
Of waiting hopes and fears,
And lo! the wedding day at last,
The goal of all the years.
With lovers' token, lovers' pledge,
My Spouse, Christ Crucified,
Has made me everlastingly
His royal queen and bride.

O little ring, you must be made
Of sterner stuff than gold
Or silver . . . 'tis with steely strength
My heart to Him you hold.
O little ring, although so small,
Wide as Infinity,
You circle round the mighty God
And bind Him down to me.

Marjorie Dexter, r.c.

My Purple Cape

I love to wear my purple cape,
It is the color of the grape
That grows in clusters on the vine,
And pressed with others makes the wine
That in the Mass can now become
The Precious Blood of God's Own Son.

Oh, then it makes me think that I
The grain of wheat must be, and die
To all the things that self loves most,
And so become a little host
In which my Christ will ever live
And glory to His Father give.

Gertrude Morton, r.c.

The Cenacle

This is the rich, green pasture of surrender,
Where grass grows greener with the passing years.
Here do we feed divinely, yet still hunger,
Rejoicing through the torrent of our tears.
Our hearts are fixed upon the Bread of Angels,
And through the earth our chant of praise goes
ringing,
Our warfare is the battle of Redemption,
Across the world we send the strong Dove winging.
Good Shepherd, keep us in pastures of surrender,
And though the mountains crumble, hold us fast,
Until some radiant midnight we are summoned,
"Behold, the Bridegroom comes!" At last, at last!

Margaret Byrne, r.c.

"As a Bride Adorned"

Isaias LXI

Let not the noise of earth's Jerusalem
Break on the stillness of the Upper Room,
Where Mary weaves the mystic wedding gown
Of longing prayer — her heart both thread
and loom.

She is the heavenly Jerusalem,
She has become the land of all desire,
God's bride-soul, waiting for Descending Love
To seal His Beauty in her by His Fire.

Catherine Carney, r.c.

The Spirit of Love

I left the cold, gray palace of my pride,
Where for a guide
I had my faltering will and intellect,
A flickering flame that every gust of air
Blew everywhere.
No casement wide
Looked out where Beauty lived without dismay,
For day by day,
Her flight was checked, her wings were caught
in bars.
She might reach stars,
But what were they without their Maker?
Clay!

I have no palace now but Love's wide lap,
Where I may hide my head and dry my tears,
Where in my fears
Feel strong Hands press and lift me sometimes,
Hear whispers in my ears,
Such tales of rapture that I catch my breath,
And feel that stars are shining in my eyes,
As in a child's, at every quick surprise
That love fulfills.
I almost see the everlasting hills.
No bars for beauty here, her boundless scope
Transcends all hope!
The torch from which we only glimpse the gleams
Transcends all dreams.

Isabelle O'Leary, r.c.

Pentecost

He came
in flame,
the Spirit Paraclete,
in love
a Dove
bound hearts at Mary's feet.
O Light!
bind mine,
that flamed it be
unto Eternity.

Alice McConville, r.c.

So Beauty Comes and Love Divine

The lake below lay dark and lifeless
Under as bleak a sky.
The air was deadly still;
In the garden not a bird
Was seen in happy flight
On nesting's sweet affairs,
From pillared elm to maple and from bowering apple
    tree
To slender poplars tall.

When suddenly
Above the lake there flashed a hundred wings
All silver lined . . .
Sound ripped the air, as wild sea gulls
In wheels and bold gyrations
Descended on the still expanse,
High dissonance resolving into ringing peace.

A chaplet of translucent pearls
Flung dexterously,
They lay with folded wings; their shining breasts
White brilliancy undreamed by ancient heraldry.

So beauty comes into our lives, and Love,
Against a background wrought by seeming chance
Or misadventure grim
To gray obscurity and shade;
Beauty more lovely for the dissonance from which
    she came,
And Pentecostal Love more rapturous
The bleaker the suspense and long,
That waited on
His coming.

Louise Manning, r.c.

Holy Mother Church

My Mother has a lovely face,
A wholly supernatural grace,
And smileth at the creepy pace
A little child can go.
    Yet sometimes in the wintry blast
    She makes me stumble on so fast,
    I chide her, 'til she shows me last,
    The winking lights of Home.
And sometimes 'neath spring's leafy bowers,
She walks with me for hours and hours,
And lets me pick the meadow flowers
To fill my pinafore.
    Or sitting in some arbor cool,
    She teaches me the golden rule
    By which the child, and eke the fool,
    Can come to Paradise.
Her voice is like a moorland stream,
Her eyes so deep, to me they seem
As peaty pools, wherein I dream
I see the face of God.
    And oh, her footstep! Oh, her hair!
    And oh, her chaste and regal air!
    Is none with her who can compare,
    God willeth her unique.
She satisfies my every need,
And like a mother-bird doth feed
Her callow nestling with the seed
Of immortality.
    And lastly, when 'tis growing late,
    She'll lead me to the garden gate,
    Where, as a Bridegroom, Christ will wait
    To claim me utterly.

Mabel Tottie, r.c.

Time after Pentecost

"Let us rejoice unto God,
the Rock of our salvation."

Matins: Invitatory
(Tuesday)

To the Creator

The evening star I loved so well
  Has set forevermore,
The surf that beat against my heart
  Now breaks on Heaven's shore.

And oh, at last, the nightingale
  Is silent now for me.
How can I think on them, my God,
  When I can think of Thee?

Margaret Byrne, r.c.

Outcast of the Air

In the summer twilight,
Silver dusk and mild,
Mary sat amid the larkspur
Singing to her Child.

Overhead a wee bird
On his homing flight,
Heard her song like bluebells ringing
Down the falling night,
    "O Beata Trinitas."
Down he swooped to Mary,
Perched upon her knee,
"Lady, I would sing that song,
Teach your song to me!"

So they sang together,
Then he wept goodbye,
Mary promised, "Sing that song
And you will never die."
    O Beata Trinitas!
Angrily his family
Cried to him one day,
"Either you will sing our song
Or you must go away."

Sorrowfully he left them,
Outcast of the air.
Year on year he looked for Mary
Calling everywhere,
    "O Beata Trinitas!"

Came another twilight,
Silver dusk and mild,
Mary sat upon a hillside
Singing to her Child.

There the wee bird found them.
Joyfully he flew,
"O sweet Lady of the Twilight,
I have longed for you."
  O Beata Trinitas!

Then he saw her white hand
Curved about His head,
Saw her grieving, saw His stillness,
Knew that He was dead.

Sobbed the wee bird, "Never
Could I sing again."
"Foolish child," said Mary softly,
"God moves through all pain,
  O Beata Trinitas!"

So in every twilight,
Silver dusk and mild,
Mary sends that wee bird winging,
Singing to each child.

Everyone may hear him,
Listen, if you will,
Singing as the day is dying,
If your heart be still,
  "O Beata Trinitas!"

Margaret Byrne, r.c.

69

Spring Song -- Indwelling

To plunge into the watchful deep of Love
That dips like pensive fingers, dripping you;
While bent to labor, flying free above,
Released from langour, breathing clearest blue.

Content, yet wounded tenderly within,
Constrained to comb the fields of flowers, the sky
Of stars; with sun, with wind, with all but sin
Companion, passive actor, I not I.

Content till summer sifts some fragrant bough,
Till autumn plucks a ripeness from the leaves,
And past or future storms snow in the now,
And sweetness drowns, gone down with one who
    grieves.

Content, for Spring, descending from above,
Repeats reviving words, "Remain in me."
And fresh-pricked Hands take back your gift of love
And flood the void marked self with Trinity.

Winifred Corrigan, r.c.

The Lady Charity

Will you answer me one question?
   Do you ever sense or see
The queen my heart is courting,
   The Lady Charity?
I have wooed her in the chapel,
   In the garden, on the stair.
She is the breath of God, you know,
   And can be everywhere.
Sometimes she hides in silence,
   Then again behind a smile,
You may see her for a second,
   If you need her just that while,
Or, minute upon minute,
   Even to a minute-mile.
And yet, for all her queenliness,
   She's childlike, gay and meek,
And I've found her favorite play to be
   The game of hide-and-seek.

Clare Gartland, r.c.

My Father's House

Did you ever build a tunnel
Through a mow of new mown hay?
Have you ever run barefooted
Through the dew at dusk of day?
Have you fingered funny folk
On a table that was dusty?
Did you ever catch red rain
In a tin can that was rusty?
Did you ever pick blackberries
Till your pail was dark and filled,
And then trip in a woodchuck hole
To have each last one spilled?
Have you made a cookie man
With wrinkled raisin eyes?
Did you ever serve your Mother
With caked mud that you called pies?
Have you ever scratched cold castles
On a frosted windowpane?
Have you ever cramped your neck
For a whirling weathervane?
Have you linked the summer fragrance
Of a June day's daisy chain?
Have you ever wandered noplace
In monotony of rain?
Have you felt the warm, silk throbbing
Of a sleeping kitten's breast?
Or found the speckled blueness
Of a jealous robin's nest?
Haven't you ever? Never? Ever?
Please forgive me if I say,
Begin to live, begin to love,
Today.

Clare Gartland, r.c.

Encounter

As ceaseless as white-crested waves at morning,
Christ's fellows press
Upon Him on the Eucharistic shore
In utter weariness;
Fagged by the futile labors of the night,
With buffeting and strife,
They fold their lives within His welcoming own,
His love and greater life . . .
Then turn, enriched by their encounter, and recede
Charged with new buoyancy
To wrestle with life's goring winds,
Despair's black tyranny . . .
To taste life's bitter brine or halcyon sweet
As He ordains,
God of the storm, Lord of tranquillity.

Louise Manning, r.c.

One Body, One Bread

The temple of God
Is flesh and bone
With wafer of Bread
For Cornerstone.

Lucille Lang, r.c.

The Carved Oak Communion Rail Speaks

Beyond Bach's vision the chorale
Played by the western wind upon my branches
Yesterday . . .
Beyond Corot's conceit
My foliage against the setting sun
At autumn's end.

Today
I lie as one by death outstripped,
An embellished memory . . .
And yet,
Against me press soft, little hands,
Toil-hardened palms,
Magenta tipped, long leisured fingers;
And left hands unaware
Of what their right have given.
Above, I hear the whispered prayer,
The breath of confidence,
The hush
Of the embrace of Christ and His beloved!

Louise Manning, r.c.

75

Passing By

"Jesus of Nazareth was passing by."

St. Luke xviii

Up and down the whole wide world,
All the livelong day,
Jesus Christ is passing by.
Speed Him on His way!

As of old in Galilee,
So 'twill ever be,
"Blessed are the clean of heart,"
They their God shall see!

All the world is full of Him,
Earth and sea and sky!
Would our hearts might sing of Him,
As He passes by!

Watch Him down the village street,
Tramping wearily;
He Who sat by Jacob's Well
Asks an alms of thee.

Flower-girls with their posies gay,
"Let me sell you one!"
Buy a flower for love of Him,
E'er the day is done.

Daisies in the meadow grass,
Poppies in the wheat,
Stones along the dusty road,
Kiss His wounded feet.

In the Blessed Sacrament,
He has come to stay!
Love could do no greater thing,
Find no better way!

Ah, then I will look for Him,
All the livelong day!
Walk with Him, and talk with Him,
Passing on His way!

Blessed be Thy passing, Lord,
Blest the eyes that see!
Jesus, bless all needy folk,
Not forgetting *me!*

Mabel Tottie, r.c.

He Is All

"What think you of Christ?"

St. Matthew XXII

What do I think of Christ, you ask?
How should I ever say,
Since He has given His life for me,
And stolen my heart away!

He is the sunlight on the sea,
The blossom on the spray,
The fruit of all earth's harvestings,
The scent of new mown hay,

The song of every singing bird,
The murmur of the breeze,
The wind that breaks the cedars,
And the humming of the bees.

He is the silence of the night,
The peace of twilight gray,
The sunset fires on snowcapped peaks,
The glory of the day!

The blessed Fruit of Mary's womb,
The Fruit of Calvary's tree,
My only Love, Christ Crucified,
Is all the world to me!

Mabel Tottie, r.c.

Proper of the Saints

" The Lord, the King of kings,
Come, let us adore,
For He indeed is the crown
of all the Saints. "

Matins: Invitatory
(All Saints)

Abandonment

In vain I tried to navigate the sea
Of holiness, avoiding reef and bar
Of sand, watch beacons on the rocks,
Compass in hand to gauge the Northern Star.
In vain I turned my sails to catch the wind;
Too strong it blew. It dashed my sinking skiff
Out on the rocks. My plans to reach the port
Had failed; a wreckage washed upon the cliff.

Oarless I sail upon the Sea of Love,
Abandoned as a gull upon its breast,
Without a chart, with Love for sails I go
Over the seas with God. That way is best!

Isabelle O'Leary, r.c.

Immaculate

Adam's seed is free from sin,
O blessed Anne and Joachim!

Thou dost not know the mystery
Omnipotence hath wrought through thee!

Pre-redeemed this child of thine
By privilege unique, sublime!

Immaculate, thy kith and kin,
O happy Anne and Joachim!

Gretchen Funck, r.c.

Fruition

O Chastity, I took your cold white heart
    And held it close to mine;
But as I held it there, mine flushed rose-red,
    The melted snow was wine.

Isabelle O'Leary, r.c.

The First Dolor

A mother, silent, young, alight with joy,
  Holds up her Babe to meet an old man's gaze.
God's prophet lives his long awaited hour,
  No longer need God stretch his span of days;
His eyes have seen Salvation clothed in flesh.
  Oh, Israel, how wonderful God's ways!

The mother faintly smiles and presses close
  Her tiny Babe with face so like her own.
He is so small, she thinks, to be so great . . .
  The Son of God, yet my own flesh and bone.
What holds Thy life for Thee, my little One?
  The angel said for sin Thou must atone.

The old man speaks to her. What words are these?
  "Thy soul a sword shall pierce." She does not weep.
Though well she knows that only through the Son
  She's holding to her breast in peaceful sleep
Can suffering touch her heart, she says no word;
  Her vow, her *fiat mihi* she will keep.

Virginia Lawrence, r.c.

The Mixed Life

The way is far and the quest is high,
I must go alone to the rim of the sky
To catch His garments passing by;
Then I must go to the market place,
And with the mirror of His grace
Reflect the beauty of His face.

Isabelle O'Leary, r.c.

The Lure of the Land

Say, lad! Hast watched the robin woo his brown
    mate in the spring?
Dost know he flaunts his flaming breast to win the
    timid thing?
Hast ever found a thrush's egg as blue as Cynthia's
    eyes?
Or glimpsed the first forget-me-not 'neath April's
    willful skies?
Hast caught the cuckoo's crazy cry 'mid hawthorn's
    drifted snow?
Or seen the plover trail her wing, lest haply thou
    shouldst know
Her darling nestling crouched so nigh? Could'st
    say where salmon leap?
Or where the red-shank finds his food? Or where
    I fold the sheep?
Hast ever risen with the lark, to scythe the summer's
    hay?
Or slept beneath the winking stars, to overtake the
    day?
Will'st never hear the ring of skates across a frozen
    pond,
Nor gaze at sunlight on the hills, and wonder what's
    beyond?
Go to! Thou little townling-child! I almost weep
    thy birth!
Thou'llt hear Death call, e'er thou hast guessed this
    paradise on earth!
Aren't scared to think that thou must lie below yon
    dankish sod,
Who'st never picked a buttercup, nor lisped the
    name of God?

Mabel Tottie, r.c.

The Annunciation

A small plain room and a girl at prayer.
Nothing there
To startle the High Priest in the court
Where doves are bought.
The drop of a wing
And a strange bright thing
Entered in.
The room became
The living flame
Lighting the darkest corners of the world.
"Fiat" was said. Its swift impact
Sundered the symbol, revealing the fact.
A head bent low,
Life leaped afresh,
The Word was made flesh,
But the High Priest slept
While the maiden kept
Locked in her heart the Beginning and End.

Isabelle O'Leary, r.c.

Peace Lies Deep

"Hail, full of grace," most radiant, most fair.
Tiberias in the noonday blaze of sun
Is not more bright, its waters hold less rare,
Less clear a light, O pure, O burning one.

"Fear not, Mary." The beating of mighty wings,
The golden figure moving across the floor,
The voice, are forms of old foreshadowings,
Signs of a world surrender will restore.

"Be it done." Fire and wind and a breaking joy,
The wild sweet plunge with God through singing
    space;
Down in your heart the dream of a Little Boy,
Who walks the earth with Heaven in His face.

There will be pain tomorrow in the Lord,
But peace lies deep beneath His shining sword.

Eileen Surles, r.c.

St. Joseph

Joseph was a quiet man, his mind was hushed in
    wonder,
His thoughts were so unearthly that words could not
    match their splendor.

The days were slow while he sawed and filed,
But the nights were swift by the sleeping Child,
And the Sabbath days with the Boy and His Mother,
The three of them knowing and loving each other.
And the years flowed by and he grew older,
And Christ was tall against Joseph's shoulder.
Side by side with his God in labor,
Not in Gethsemane, not on Mount Thabor.
When his task was done, with no hesitating
He quietly slipped into Limbo—waiting—

His questions unanswered, his longings unheeded,
For Joseph was satisfied not to be needed.

Margaret Byrne, r.c.

Blissful Maiden

I saw a blissful maiden
(with hair like ripening corn)
a'swaddling her Infant
that was but newly born.
God willed her maid and mother
she was so very fair!
(There is no gold in Jewry
like the gold of Mary's hair.)

I saw a blissful maiden
(like woodland pools, her eyes)
a'singing to her Dearling
the songs of Paradise.
God loved the happy mother
she was so lowly-wise!
(There are no pools in Jewry
like the pools of Mary's eyes.)

I saw a blissful maiden
whose tears like dew distilled,
a'mingling with the blood-drops
that from her Youngling spilled.
God would that lustral water
with wine should flow blood-red!
(There are no tears in Jewry
like the tears that Mary shed.)

I saw a blissful maiden
(she bore her like a queen)
a'standing by her Nursling
upon a hilltop green.
Her little Lamb she offered,
God's Paschal Lamb, I ween!
(There is no queen in Jewry
like to Mary, Heaven's Queen.)

I saw a blissful maiden
crowned as a royal bride,
up-raised on a dais,
her dear Son by her side.
God's meek and humble handmaid
had climbed Love's winding stair!
(There are no crowns in Jewry
like the crown on Mary's hair.)

Mabel Tottie, r.c.

Response

Oh, why may I no longer see Thy face?
Why from Thy beauty must I live withdrawn,
To walk down starless nights where shadows are,
I who have seen the glory of the dawn?

On lonely shorelands worn by thunderous waves,
A beacon's sudden flashing through the dark,
Because of its eclipse at intervals,
Gives surer guidance to the straitened bark.

Isabelle O'Leary, r.c.

Saint Paul

I love Thee, God, but with no love of mine
    For I have none to give.
I love Thee, Lord, but all the love is Thine
    For in Thy Life I live.
I am as nothing, and rejoice to be
    Emptied and lost and swallowed up in Thee.
Thou, Lord, art all Thy children need
    And there is none beside.
From Thee the streams of life proceed,
    In Thee the blest abide.
Oh, Fount of Love and all sufficing grace,
    Our Source, our Center, our Abiding Place.

Eliza Stickney, r.c.

An Apology to Saint Paul

Saint Paul exhorted runners in the race
To keep apace
With all the laws that regulate that sport.
With muscles taut
And limbs well oiled and spare,
To be aware
Of all the hidden obstacles that lay
Across their way.

I prefer to enter in the run
With little children free and full of fun,
Unmindful of all laws, save one.
With flying ringlets and with eager eyes
Sure of the prize
Because they know
That fast or slow
Their Father's arms are there to lift them high
Up to the sky.

The only requisite to win that race
Is hidden in the secret of His face,
And folded in the prison of His grasp,
Never to unclasp
Their hold,
And never to grow old.

I can only run apace
In a little children's race.

Isabelle O'Leary, r.c.

94

The Holy Sacrifice

"Comprehensus sum a Christo."
Philippians III

Now looms the summit of your adoration.
Not yours the way of neophytes less strong
Whose Offertory is a lifetime long.
But come, the chosen to the Consecration,
Come to this utmost limit of compassion.
Mingle the years' pure water with the wine,
Knowing it has a destiny divine
To be the Gift Incarnate Love must fashion.

So falls the Solemn Silence—oh, be still!
There is nothing now that is not sacrificed,
Nothing that is not gathered into Christ,
Nothing that is not yielded to His Will,

Nothing that does not yearn exultantly
For the long Thanksgiving of Eternity.

Margaret Byrne, r.c.

Magdalen's Last Lover

"The Son of man is come to save that which was lost."

St. Matthew XVIII

Magdalen's fingers were long and white,
And her emerald glowed into the candlelight.
The air with her perfume was thick, was thick,
But Magdalen's heart was sick, was sick.
"Is there anything good? Is there anything true? . . .
Nazareth's Jesus? . . ." the strange thought grew.
But shame swept up like a rising tide,
Bent down the dark head, and Magdalen cried.

Magdala's streets were crowded and gay,
But many heads turned as she went on her way,
Astonished to see her, the sinner, in tears!
Their laughter crashed thunder in Magdalen's ears.
But what would it matter, if Christ should be kind?
"God, don't let me remember . . ." But Christ she
must find.
She sought Him. She found Him. She knew it was
He.
She entered the house of the Pharisee.
And oh, Christ's face was grave and sweet,
And Magdalen's tears washed His dusty feet.

Lazarus sickened. His sisters were numb.
But Jesus loved Lazarus. Jesus would come.
So they trusted and waited and watched as his side,
But long before Jesus came, Lazarus died.
Martha and Mary held tight to each other.
Christ sent no word, so they buried their brother.

Heartbroken, Mary thought, "Where can Christ be?"
Then, "The Master is come and calleth for thee."
And the light in her eyes dimmed the noon sun
    above,
What heart can break that has Christ for its Love?

But all through the valleys and highways He trod,
A suffering world laughed at the pity of God.
They hunted Him east, and they hunted Him west,
And Magdalen's heart was a stone in her breast.
Fear hung on those days like a late autumn chill.
Only Mary, His Mother, was smiling and still.

It was the springtime of thirty-three,
And out from the green hills of Galilee,
Into Jerusalem Jesus came;
And the word went round like a wind-driven flame,
Almighty Redeemer, meekness His power.
"For this cause came I to this hour."
They led Him away from Gethsemane.
They took Him and killed Him on Calvary;
And through that long day while His tired heart
    beat,
Magdalen stayed at His bleeding feet . . .
But this was her joy as the hot tears ran,
"The Son of God is the Son of man."

Margaret Byrne, r.c.

97

"Sicut Incensum"

Psalm CXL

There was a time, when on the hills at dawn
I swung my heart, a censer to the skies,
As mists of blue against the opal skies,
I saw the incense of my laughter rise.

Then sorrow came. It broke the jesting heart,
And of its fragments built a cloister where
From censers swung by angels down dark ways
Blue clouds of incense rise to God in prayer.

Isabelle O'Leary, r.c.

Idyl

A subtle perfume in the air,
A silken swish upon the stair
Of Simon's house, and Magdalen's hair
Soft ruffling in the breeze,
  Which on a sudden open blows
  The lattices, to half-disclose
  The Master's face . . . whereby she knows
  Her scarlet sins He sees.

A memory: "As white as snow . . ."
"Who feedeth where the lilies grow . . ."
She turns, in utter shame, as though
To weep beneath the trees.
  Instead, she spills her spikenard sweet,
  Lets fall her tears upon His feet,
  And with her hair (like rippling wheat)
  Most fitly wipeth these.

A breath of heaven in the air,
A rush of angels on the stair,
An aureole round Magdalen's hair,
Soft ruffling in the breeze,
  Which on the instant clangeth to
  The lattices. Her soul made new,
  Fair as a garden wet with dew,
  Is all the Master sees.

Mabel Tottie, r.c.

99

S avior mine, let me ....

U se Thy ....

S trength, then my soul ....

C an sing ....

I rrevocable ....

P ledge of ....

E verything.

Clare Gartland, r.c.

This Rapture

There is no turning from You now, my Lord,
You hold me fast. I gave myself, and love
Plunging like wind and fire from above
Has captured me. Your will is my reward.

No singing voice can draw my heart away,
And sunlight on the hills is less to me
Than spray that blows above an inland sea.
Even the dreams are gone. I am Your prey.

The darkest night may beat against my eyes,
The wildest storm may crash above my head,
Thunder and lightning till the birds are fled.
I shall not stir, I shall not hear their cries.

There is nothing now but the deep recurring breath,
My Lord, my Lord, this rapture looks on death!

Eileen Surles, r.c.

Suscipe

(A Little Way of the Cross)

I.   Take my little silences
     As token of my love.
II. Take my generosities,
     The over-and-above.
III. Take my falls as weakness,
     Not as sins of will.
IV. Take my fears to Mary,
     For her eyes to still.
V.   Take me for a Simon,
     Oh . . . for anyone,
VI. Take me for a veil whereon
     All may see God's Son.
VII. Take my many lapses,
     And each new beginning,
VIII. Take my words and make them
     Beacons for the sinning.
IX. Take all my exhaustion,
     It is love in labor,
X.   Take my pure desires,
     Of Thine let them savor.
XI. Take my heart and nail it
     To Thy sacred feet,
XII. Take each "Consummatum est"
     That my days repeat.
XIII. Take my body, Jesus,
     Living . . . and then dead,
XIV. Take my faith in glory,
     Thou hast risen, as Thou said.

Clare Gartland, r.c.

102

Finding Her

"He that shall find me, shall find life."

Proverbs VIII

Trouble me not with anguished thoughts of death;
Now in a cloud of hope I make my dwelling.
Think you I build my castle on a breath,
Or find the blossoms of frail dust compelling?
Our Lady in her summer passed my way,
Hushed in the Incarnation's afterglow,
From the surrender of Ascension Day
Into a cloud of hope I watched her go.

To her sweet mysteries I am appointed,
And from the sacred scripture of her heart
A deeper knowledge comes with love anointed.
I shall come Home to her when I depart!
Trouble me not with your dark dreams of death;
My castle is not built upon a breath.

Margaret Byrne, r.c.

"Assumpta Est Maria"

She who had been a living heaven
    For God of old,
Came, on a day, to death's dark portal,
    As sunset's gold

Glinted on cornfields white to harvest,
    (Ah! fact sublime!)
Fields that the Mind of God had thought of,
    Ere dawn of time.

Saw she, in dream, her dear Son, walking
    Through yellow wheat?
Fain would I think she caught His footfall,
    And accents sweet:

"Leave all things else, and come, My Mother,
    Possess your Son!
Death has no sting, the grave no terrors,
    My stainless one!"

Clothed with the sun, the moon beneath her,
    Halts she a pace;
Gazing at earth with wistful pity,
    Till Christ's fair face

Shines through the mists that hid Him from her
    These many years!
Roses and lilies breathe their fragrance
    Through drenching tears!

Mabel Tottie, r.c.

The Assumption

Oh, what a lovely journey
Was planned for Our Lady that day,
When on a summer morning,
She traveled far away.

Up from the meadow of flowers,
Singing like bells all around,
She rose like a cloud in the dawning
Up from the radiant mound.

Leaving the irised hilltops
And Lebanon gleaming afar,
Up through the lucent ether,
Up past the morning star.

And oh, what an end to the journey,
Where all journeys end at the last,
The meeting of lovers forever,
When the dim farthest outpost is passed.

Isabelle O'Leary, r.c.

Retreat Schedule

Dearest Lady, your procession
Has been canceled
Due to rain,
And reasons for unanswered prayer
Our hastening thoughts
Detain.
Do you prefer abandonment
To living lanes of song
And lanterns breathing praise along
The hem of dusk?
In between the raindrops,
We conclude you must!

Clare Gartland, r.c.

To a Novice Reading Saint Bernard

The light falls on St. Bernard's words
    Penned long ago
Beside a flickering flame of oil
    In stern Clairvaux.
Like knotted scourges now they lash
    And bid us stay
To weigh our threefold nothingness —
    Worms of a day.

Again, mellifluous they pour
    Out on the air,
Exotic of the flowery paths
    Of Eden fair;
Recalling Nazareth obscure,
    Where none the less
Bright Gabriel from Heaven was sent
    For Mary's "Yes."

Oh, cadence suave, so hast thy balm
    My soul's depths stirred,
No greater fullness may she await
    Save God's own word.

Louise Manning, r.c.

Our Lady's Nativity

This was the lovely beginning. This was the day
Leaping from darkness at last into wind, into sun,
That heard the first sound of your feet on the way,
O most pure, O immaculate one.

This was the sparkling source of a radiant stream,
Flowing like music between the dim banks of your
    love;
The years gathered beauty and strength from the
    dream
Dropping to you from above.

This was the start of a strange and ineffable grace
That fashioned your will to the infinite Will of the
    Lord.
There was no fear, no surprise in your face,
When Simeon spoke of a sword.

Eileen Surles, r.c.

The Sign of the Cross

In the name of the Father,
Who made the world,
Let banners of intellect
Be unfurled.

And of the Son,
Whose Blood is cost
For all Adam lost,
Let wills be one.

And of the Holy Ghost,
Who sanctifies,
From eyes and sighs
Let love arise.
Let nothing be lost.

Amen.

Clare Gartland, r.c.

Hymn to Mother Therese

I

Hear the hearts that beg for goodness,
Hear the prayers that never cease
For a world that's lost in turmoil,
Bring that world a lasting peace.

II

Show the world how to surrender
To the Will of God Most High,
Teach us all that earthly glories
Count for naught beyond the skies.

III

From the Cenacle in Heaven
Guard us with a Mother's care,
Keep us all united closely
In our work and in our prayer.

Refrain

Mother Therese, oh, hear us calling,
Mother Therese, thy children plead,
Mother Therese, oh, lean thou toward us,
Lend thy help unto our need.

Ida Barlow, r.c.

To Mother Therese

What wisdom drew you to this road of fire,
When in an Ardeche sunrise long ago,
The feet of love outran the drifting snow,
In search of the White Furnace of Desire?
What brave surrender to Omnipotence,
Won you His strength along this burning way
That ended in the ashes of the day,
Upon a mount of myrrh and frankincense?

That darkened hill your refuge from the night,
O Calvary of loneliness, O loss!
Another victim dies upon the cross,
Certain of death's baptism into light,
Crying the lover's answer to defeat,
Nothing is so easy, nothing so sweet!

Margaret Byrne, r.c.

The Gift

Through myriad ranks of burning seraphim,
Up to the very throne of God she goes,
Unwavering with utter trusting love,
To place there at His feet a small white rose.

Around His throne eternal harmonies
Are swelling from a thousand angel bands.
He heeds them not, He only sees the rose,
Still throbbing from the touch of human hands.

Isabelle O'Leary, r.c.

Sister Agnes of Jesus

(Pauline Martin
1861-1951)

Prioress beloved of God and men, your name
The generations yet to come will hold
In benediction. For without your word
The *History of a Soul* had not been told.

Love was your primary lesson to Therese,
The golden-haired, who climbed upon your knee
To learn heaven's ways. In Carmel she would find
Love's silences poignant austerity.

And when the early sunset came to close
Her days, we hear your word, her heart to prove,
"In the evening of life we shall be judged, ah, yes!
Not by great deeds, but according to our love."

Louise Manning, r.c.

An Autumn Rose

When Autumn winds are blowing through the trees
The first sad notes of nature's obsequies,
And elm trees lift their arms of flaming fires
In murmurous glades where burn earth's funeral
    pyres;
When russet leaves hang aimless in the air,
And faded roses mock the hedgerows bare;
When lonely sea-birds farewell anthems sing
To swallows gone to seek another Spring,
One fair sweet rose with shell-like petals curled
(An Autumn rosebud in a dying world)
Lifts up its head in face of death to sing,
Through Autumn's wail, a canticle of Spring.

Isabelle O'Leary, r.c.

The Canticle of the Sun

Like the sound of many waters
The seraphs' voices soared
Around the throne of heaven,
And the Lamb of God adored.

But listening they wondered
As their chanting rose and fell,
For a voice from earth was swelling
Their mighty canticle.

Then flashed the word like lightning:
"More glorious yet, our hymn—
The Poor Man of Assisi
Sings with the seraphim!"

Louise Manning, r.c.

Castle of Silence

Silence is Your castle, O my King.
You walk its sunny corridors in peace,
Untroubled by the conflict voices bring,
Secure against the chaos sounds release.

You pace its windy battlements by night,
Head in the stars, cloak against the moon,
Seeking the Wisdom that is born of Light,
Patient in this: Folly is over soon.

You open leaded casements to the dawn,
An angel speeds across the flaming skies,
Bearing the words of love, from silence drawn,
Spoken by God to man in Paradise.

Your castle dreams forever on its hill.
O tongue, O mind, O heart, be still, be still.

Eileen Surles, r.c.

Children of an Older Growth

"Oh, take my hand, I cannot go alone
Up that dark stairway, come, I am afraid."
I clasped the child's frail hand within my own,
We climbed that Stygian stairway undismayed.

A timid child in all but years, I turn,
Afraid to trace the perilous path alone
That cuts the abyssmal caverns of my soul,
To place a trembling hand within your own.

Isabelle O'Leary, r.c.

Detachment

Through windows of my heart I saw them fly,
My loves, those beauteous things I called my own.
Afraid to meet the loneliness within,
I turned to find Love on the empty throne.

Isabelle O'Leary, r.c.

My Father's Will

Come into My Father's Will and shut the door.
Is it little and dark at first to your startled eyes,
Filled with the brightness of sun on the forest floor?
It will grow large and light as you grow wise.

Come away from that open window, come away.
There is nothing outside but the restless crying of
    birds,
The rushing of streams that plunge to a distant bay,
And the wistful, passing sound of human words.

Nothing for you, nothing to hold your heart.
I am waiting for you in a chair beside the fire,
Come into My arms and the long sweet dream will
    start,
Dream without anguish, dream without desire.

Hush, hush, this is no longer Time.
The years do not matter now, let the striving cease,
The clock on the mantel shelf has a different chime.
Nothing is real but the mighty rhythm of peace.

Eileen Surles, r.c.

121

Christ the King

(A Little Way of the Cross)

I. King of Kings, O muted Word,
    Very God and Man concurred;

II. Thorn-crowned, sceptre carved in sin,
    Robed in blame of all His kin;

III. Government His shoulders' weight,
    Staggers, falls beneath man's hate.

IV. Rules away heart's satisfaction
    To embrace a jeered detraction.

V. Power disguised implores of weakness
    Strength to garb its royal meekness.

VI. Veil of linen takes His seal
    Kingly kindness to reveal.

VII. Stoops Himself to raise again
    Princes fallen prey to sin.

VIII. Promulgates the Truth's compassion,
    Courtiers of love to fashion.

IX. Fallen, triples the assurance
    Of His Mercy's long endurance.

X. Naked, for the mob's hard stare,
    His ermine wrap but cloud and air.

XI. Blood His wide dominion's pledge,
    Flowing back unto hell's edge.

XII. Raised on high, hands fixed in blessing,
    Love, unmatched in time, confessing.

XIII. Tearfully His Queen-in-waiting
    Takes the crown of man's cruel plaiting,

XIV. Visioning the Crown of Glory
    Telling evermore Love's story.

Clare Gartland, r.c.

122

Elegy

When I am dead, and put to bed
Beneath the red rose tree,
Then will the Church, my Mother, bring
Her hallowed gifts, and softly sing
A lullaby to me:

"My cherished child, may Christ so mild,
In pity bend o'er thee,
And may the saints in long rows stand,
And may the angels, hand-in-hand,
Run out to welcome thee!

And when earth's fears and sorry tears
Have all been kissed away,
Then may thy soul, at God's right hand,
A blissful bride, take up her stand,
In holiday array!"

Mabel Tottie, r.c.

No Other Sound

The music of Your Will is breaking thunder,
The whip of lightning cracked across the sky,
Rain pouring down upon the ancient plunder,
The havoc, the pillage, of winds roaring by.

The music of Your Will is summer sunlight,
A golden cloak upon the forest floor,
The quiet fall of water, and the spun flight
Of inland birds that seek a far-off shore.

The music of Your Will is distant crying,
A small child lost, wandering in the snow,
The landmarks hidden, and the short day flying,
Night coming down and a long way to go.

Many hear a different music pound.
My Lord, my Lord, there is no other sound.

Eileen Surles, r.c.

The Kingdom of God

I sought Him on the highway,
    pilgrim-wise,

With script and staff, in
    sandals carefully shod.

I found Him not. Once,
    stripped of all, I went

Down in my heart. Lo! There
    I found my God.

Isabelle O'Leary, r.c.

The Religious of the Cenacle conduct Retreat Houses for Women in Belgium, Brazil, France, Holland, Italy, Madagascar, Switzerland, and the following English-speaking countries.

CANADA

318 Lawrence Avenue East
Toronto 12, Ontario

3689 Selkirk Street
Vancouver, British Columbia

ENGLAND

Grayshott, Hindhead, Surrey

7 Lance Lane, Wavertree
Liverpool 15

33 West Heath Road, Hempstead
London N.W. 3

28 Alexandra Road S.
Manchester 16

IRELAND

Military Road
Killiney, County Dublin

NEW ZEALAND

268 W. Tamaki Road
Auckland E. 2

136 Woburn Road
Lower Hutt

UNITED STATES

200 Lake Street
Boston 35, Massachusetts

5340 Fair Oaks Boulevard
Carmichael, California

513 Fullerton Parkway
Chicago 14, Illinois

11600 Longwood Drive
Chicago 43, Illinois

Lake Ronkonkoma
Long Island, New York

George Hill Road
Lancaster, Massachusetts

Wadsworth Street
Middletown, Connecticut

3288 North Lake Drive
Milwaukee 11, Wisconsin

Mount Kisco, New York

River Road
New Brunswick, New Jersey

693 East Avenue
Rochester 7, New York

Route 1
Rosharon, Texas

900 Spoede Road
St. Louis 24, Missouri

Warrenville, Illinois

17314 Wayzata Boulevard
Wayzata, Minnesota